CONTENTS

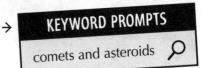

PS **Interested in primary sources? Look for this icon.**
Use a smartphone or tablet app to scan the QR code and explore more!
You can find a list of URLs on the Resources page.

If the QR code doesn't work, try searching the Internet with
the Keyword Prompts to find other helpful sources.

→ **KEYWORD PROMPTS**

comets and asteroids 🔍

66 MILLION YEARS AGO: An asteroid slams into Earth and is thought to have led to the loss of 80 percent of life on Earth, including dinosaurs.

240 BCE: Chinese astronomers are the first to record what is later named Halley's Comet.

1070s CE: Halley's Comet is embroidered on the Bayeux Tapestry.

1577: Danish astronomer Tycho Brahe makes careful measurements of a comet's path, leading him to believe that a comet's orbit extends beyond the moon.

1759: The comet returns on March 13, as predicted by Edmond Halley, and is named after him, Halley's Comet.

1786: German astronomer Caroline Herschel becomes the first woman to discover a comet. She goes on to find seven more.

1801: Giuseppe Piazzi discovers the first known asteroid, Ceres, between the orbits of Mars and Jupiter.

1833: The Leonid meteor storm amazes sky watchers in the United States.

1847: Maria Mitchell discovers a new comet.

1898: Gustav Witt discovers the asteroid Eros, which is one of the largest asteroids ever found near Earth.

1891: Max Wolf becomes the first person to discover an asteroid using photography.

1920: The world's largest meteorite, the Hoba Meteorite, is discovered by a farmer in Namibia, Africa.

1943: Kenneth Edgeworth suggests that there is a disc of comets beyond Neptune's orbit.

1950: Jan Oort predicts that there is a huge cloud of comets beyond the sun.

1951: Gerard Kuiper suggests that short-period comets lie outside the orbit of Neptune.

2014: *Rosetta* becomes the first spacecraft to touch down on the surface of a comet.

2012: *Dawn* becomes the first probe to orbit objects in the asteroid belt between Mars and Jupiter.

1985: The *International Cometary Explorer, ICE,* becomes the first spacecraft to fly through the tail of a comet.

2006: The International Astronomical Union reclassifies Pluto and Ceres as dwarf planets.

1986: Several space probes are launched to study Halley's Comet.

2006: *Hayabusa* becomes the first probe to land, collect samples, and take off from an asteroid.

1991: The *Galileo* spacecraft obtains the first up-close images of an asteroid (Gaspra) and a first moon orbiting an asteroid.

2005: Astronomers find the largest Kuiper belt object, the asteroid Eris.

1992: David Jewitt and Jane Luu discover the first Kuiper belt object.

2004: The spacecraft *Rosetta* begins its journey to rendezvous with the comet 67P/Churyumov-Gerasimenko.

JULY 16–22 1994: Fragments of the comet Shoemaker-Levy 9 crash into Jupiter, leaving massive dark scars.

1998: The Near Earth Object Program begins, tracking asteroids and comets that could be a hazard to Earth.

2001: The *Near Earth Asteroid Rendezvous (NEAR) Shoemaker* space probe lands on the asteroid Eros.

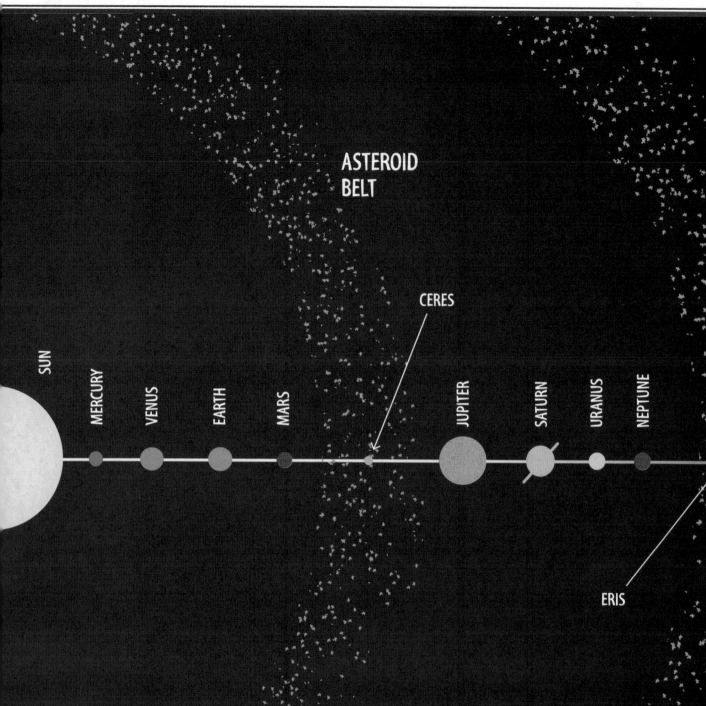

ASTEROID
BELT

CERES

SUN

MERCURY

VENUS

EARTH

MARS

JUPITER

SATURN

URANUS

NEPTUNE

ERIS

OORT
CLOUD

PLUTO

ALPHA
CENTAURI

KUIPER
BELT

INTRODUCTION

LET'S EXPLORE COMETS AND ASTEROIDS!

• • • • • • • • •

Would you like to be part of an amazing adventure? The sun has set. Look up! It's time to explore the solar system!

• •

A magical world of stars ripples across the night. Eight planets and millions of asteroids orbit around the sun. There are also visitors to our night sky that do not act like any other objects we can see. They look like fuzzy balls of light. Some of them have lizard-like tails. They are called comets.

WORDS TO KNOW

solar system: a family of eight planets and their moons that orbit the sun.

asteroid: a small rocky object that orbits the sun.

orbit: the path an object in space takes around a star, planet, or moon.

comet: a ball of ice and dust that orbits the sun.

1

crater: a large hole in the ground caused by the impact of something such as a piece of an asteroid or a bomb.

celestial body: a star, planet, moon, or other object in space, such as an asteroid or comet.

astronomy: the study of the universe, especially the celestial bodies.

astronomer: a person who studies the stars, planets, and other objects in space.

WORDS ⓣⓞ KNOW

Comets and asteroids have stories to tell. These stories are about the history of the solar system. You'll hear these stories as you zip through time and space with *Explore Comets and Asteroids!*

This book will take you from the outer edges of the solar system to massive **craters** on Earth. You'll ride on a comet's tail. You'll fly by a huge, donut-shaped band of asteroids that orbit the sun between Mars and Jupiter. Many thousands of asteroids call the asteroid belt home. Sometimes, chips off these asteroids and other **celestial bodies** fall to Earth with a thunderous clap.

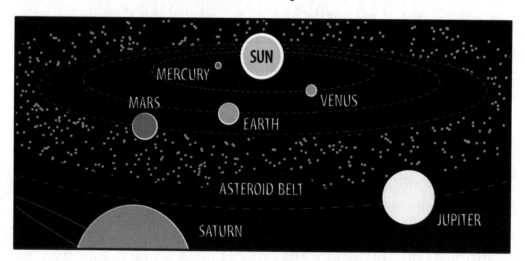

As you travel through these pages, you'll study **astronomy** and meet famous **astronomers** from ancient times. These astronomers were curious about unusual events they saw in the sky and wrote down their observations.

GOOD SCIENCE PRACTICES

Every good scientist keeps a science journal! As you read this book and do the activities, record your observations in a scientific method worksheet, like the one shown here. Scientists use the scientific method to keep their experiments organized.

Step	Example
1. Question: What are we trying to find out? What problem are we trying to solve?	Can your eyes adjust to see the night sky?
2. Research: What information is already known?	Books at the town library say that to adjust your eyes to the night sky, keep them closed for five minutes before sky watching.
3. Hypothesis/Prediction: What do we think the answer will be?	I think my eyes will adjust to the night sky.
4. Equipment: What supplies are we using?	Science journal, flashlight, timer
5. Method: What procedure are we following?	Go outside after dark. Look up and observe. Turn off your flashlight and close your eyes for five minutes. Open eyes and look up.
6. Results: What happened and why?	What is different when you look up the second time? Can you see more things in the night sky?

Each chapter of this book begins with a question to help guide your exploration of space. Keep the question in your mind as you read the chapter. At the end of each chapter, use your science journal to record your thoughts and answers.

? INVESTIGATE!

Do people worry about comets and asteroids today the way they did in historical times? Why or why not?

WORDS ⏍ KNOW

BCE: put after a date, BCE stands for Before Common Era and counts down to zero. CE stands for Common Era and counts up from zero. These nonreligious terms correspond to BC and AD. This book was printed in 2017 CE.

archaeologist: a scientist who studies ancient people and their cultures through the objects they left behind.

atmosphere: the blanket of air surrounding Earth.

For example, Chinese astronomers kept detailed records. One famous record dates to the fourth century BCE. The book is called the *Silk Atlas of Comets*. For more than 2,000 years, the book lay buried until archaeologists rediscovered it in 1973. The pages contain more than 300 years of comet records. There are descriptions of 29 comets.

Did You Know?

Once a year, an asteroid roughly the size of a car burns up in Earth's atmosphere!

The ancient astronomers thought that some comets looked like brooms or pheasants with long-tails. They also thought that a comet's appearance could be linked to events on Earth. What were these events? They included the death of a general, small and large battles, and natural disasters, such as floods.

In reality, none of this was true. But people from many different cultures believe that comets and asteroids were mysterious messages from the gods.

telescope: a tool used to see objects that are far away.

probe: a spaceship or other device used to explore outer space.

WORDS ⊕ KNOW

Today, our information about comets and asteroids is not limited to what we can see with the naked eye. Modern astronomers use powerful telescopes and probes. They perform experiments in space to unlock the secrets of comets and asteroids.

WHY DID THE STAR GET A PARKING TICKET?

It forgot to pay the meteor!

Learning about comets and asteroids means asking lots of questions. What are they? Where do they come from? How old are they? Are any headed to Earth? In *Explore Comets and Asteroids!*, you'll discover what comets and asteroids are made of and how they formed. You'll read about the spacecraft created to study them. You'll learn of one probe that flew right through a comet's tail. You'll read about another that landed on an asteroid.

You'll also learn about a daring National Aeronautics and Space Administration (NASA) project to move an asteroid into a new orbit around the moon. Along the way, you'll get to do fun experiments and projects. You'll also hear some silly jokes and cool facts.

Are you ready to rock out? Don't delay. This space journey began more than 4.6 billion years ago. It's time to explore comets and asteroids!

?

CONSIDER AND DISCUSS

It's time to consider and discuss: Do people worry about comets and asteroids today the way they did in historical times? Why or why not?

THE GREAT SCARE

One hundred years ago, people still didn't know much about comets. The average person did not yet understand what a comet was. When they heard that Halley's Comet was returning in 1910, they panicked! What was so scary about a comet that astronomers had been tracking for hundreds of years?

As comets move closer to the sun, they grow a massive tail of gas and dust. Newspapers incorrectly reported that Halley's tail contained a deadly poison that would kill anyone who breathed it in. People believed the stories. Rumors spread that the world was coming to an end.

Did You Know?

In 1786, Caroline Herschel became the first woman to discover a comet. She would find seven more comets during the next 10 years.

Astronomers tried to calm the public. They explained that they had nothing to fear. People did not believe them. They prepared for the worst. Some locked themselves in their homes. They sealed doors and windows. They bought anti-comet pills from sellers who claimed that the pills would keep them safe. Of course, the pills were just a cheap trick.

When the comet came, no one was poisoned and nothing terrible happened. Many people felt foolish and others thought that the pills had worked. For some, it taught them the lesson that science is important. Without science, people would not learn what is true and what is false.

PS You can read a newspaper article that warns the public of the dangers of the comet here. Do you think the writers were being responsible?

KEYWORD PROMPTS

Library of Congress Halley's Comet Call 🔍

BE A SKY WATCHER

SUPPLIES

* science journal and pencil
* ruler

It is not possible for you to observe a comet every night, but you can observe the moon and the stars. In this activity, you are going to observe the stars during the period of a week using only your eyes. Write down your observations and draw pictures in your science journal.

1 Divide one page of your journal into eight equal sections. In the first section, write down your prediction to the question, "Will the stars appear in the same place every night?"

2 Observe the stars at the same time in the evening for the next seven nights. Refer to the scientific method worksheet in this book to help guide your study.

3 Write down your observations using one square for each evening. Note the sizes, colors, and positions of these celestial bodies.

4 At the end of the seven days, look at your results. What happened? Was your prediction correct? Why or why not? If you did this experiment again, is there anything you would change?

TRY THIS! Repeat the above experiment, but this time observe the moon each evening for four weeks. Do you think the moon will be the same shape each evening? Why or why not? Will the moon be in the same position each evening? Why or why not?

PROJECT!

SCIENCE SCROLL

The earliest sky watchers kept records of their observations. You are going to make a scroll designed after ones Chinese astronomers once used. You can use this scroll to draw your night sky observations!

SUPPLIES

* newspaper
* 7 sheets of white paper (8.5 by 11 inches)
* instant coffee
* teaspoon measure
* small bowl
* shallow tray
* sponge
* clear tape
* tinfoil
* 2 jumbo straws or skewers

1 Before you begin, cover your work area with several layers of newspaper. Lay out the sheets of white paper on the covered work area.

2 Mix 2 teaspoons of instant coffee with 1 cup of warm water in the small bowl. Pour this mixture into the shallow tray.

3 Dip each sheet of paper briefly into the tray and then place it on the newspaper to dry. Do not stack the sheets. To make the color more intense, dip the sponge into the coffee mixture and dab the paper again here and there. Let your paper dry completely.

THEN & NOW

THEN: In 1608, a German-Dutch lens maker named Hans Lippershey invented the telescope. Astronomers began using it to study the sky.

NOW: The world's most powerful telescope, which is capable of looking 13 billion light years away, is being built on the summit of Mauna Kea in Hawaii.

4 Tape the short sides of the dried paper sheets together to make a long scroll. Tape a straw to either end.

5 Make mini comets and asteroids out of the tinfoil. Draw them in pencil on the dull side of the foil. Cut out the images and tape them flat on the jumbo straws, covering up the edges of the paper.

6 Roll in the top and bottom sheets to make a scroll. You can use your scroll over time to draw the stars and planets and other things you see in the night sky.

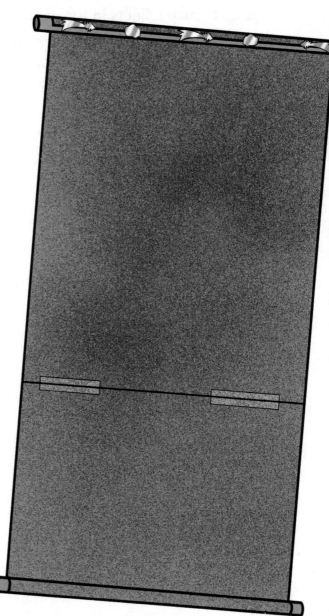

QUADRANT

Since ancient times, people have relied on their eyes to study the sky. They also built tools such as quadrants to map objects in the night sky. The quadrant provided them with the position and angle of an object, such as a comet. You can turn a piece of cardboard into a quadrant and conduct your own investigations.

1 Trace around the mixing bowl on the scrap paper and cut out the circle. Fold the circle in half and in half again. Use scissors to cut out one of these fourths. This is your quadrant template.

2 Place the paper template on the cereal box and trace it. Cut out your quadrant.

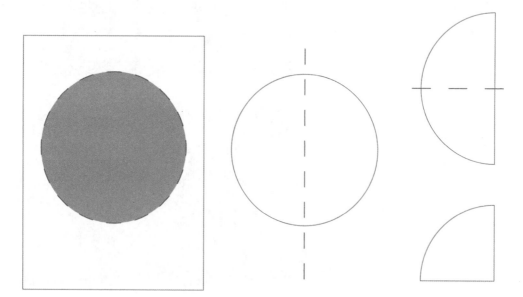

PROJECT!

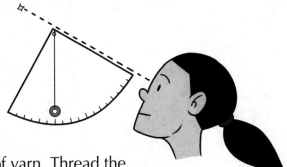

3 Use the protractor and the ruler to mark the degrees on your quadrant.

4 Cut out a ruler's length of yarn. Thread the end through the large bead and secure it with a knot. Tape the opposite end of the yarn to the quadrant's point.

5 Hold your quadrant upright with the zero mark toward your nose and the 90-degree mark farther away. Line the quadrant up with a star. The yarn will hang down vertically. It will show you the number of degrees that the star is to the **horizon**. Write down in your science scroll what is happening and your observations.

TRY THIS! On a moonless night, use your quadrant to find the North Star. First, locate the star pattern known as the Big Dipper. Notice the two stars on the outer cup section of the Big Dipper. With your eyes, draw a line from the star at the top of the open cup directly to the North Star. Hold your quadrant as you did above with the bead hanging down straight. Point the quadrant at the North Star. Press the string against the quadrant and write this number down in your science journal. This number is the **latitude** of your position. You can check your results at the United States Geographical Society. Visit this website and follow the instructions.

WORDS ⓣⓞ KNOW

quadrant: an instrument used to measure the height of the planets, moon, or stars.

horizon: the line in the distance where the land or sea seems to meet the sky.

latitude: the angle of a location from the equator. The latitude is 0 degrees at the equator and 90 degrees at the North and South Poles.

KEYWORD PROMPTS

USGS Earth explorer 🔍

CHAPTER 1

ALL ABOUT ASTEROIDS

• •

There are hundreds of thousands of rocks hurtling through space. These are called asteroids. Asteroids are chunks of rock and metal. Scientists estimate our solar system is home to billions of asteroids! Every day, new ones are discovered. A few asteroids are larger than mountains. Some are so tiny that powerful telescopes can barely seem them!

• •

Imagine hitching a flight on a spacecraft to see asteroids. As you travel through our solar system, you might be surprised at the asteroids you encounter. Asteroids come in many different shapes. They remind people of potatoes, bowling pins, and dog bones.

INVESTIGATE!

Why do asteroids come in many different shapes and sizes?

Asteroids are not usually round like planets because their gravity is much weaker. On Earth, for example, gravity is so strong that everything is always being pulled toward the planet's center. This is why Earth looks like a giant marble from space.

But on asteroids, larger rocks can resist the weak gravity. They stick out at all sorts of angles like arms and legs.

Astronomers place asteroids into groups called families. Each family of asteroids shares a similar orbit. There are three major asteroid families. They are the main asteroid belt, the Trojan asteroids, and the near-Earth asteroids.

gravity: a force that pulls all matter together, including planets, moons, and stars.

main asteroid belt: an area of space between the orbits of Mars and Jupiter where most asteroids are found.

Trojan asteroids: asteroids that share their orbits with larger objects in the solar system, such as planets.

near-Earth asteroids: asteroids that travel along orbits close to Earth.

WORDS TO KNOW

BOO!

An asteroid named 2015 TB145 once gave astronomers a scare. This massive, 2,000-foot-wide asteroid is about twice the size of a sports stadium. In October 2015, it flew by Earth looking as though it was wearing a Halloween mask. The asteroid looked like a skull! This led astronomers to nickname it "Spooky."

PS

You can see what the astronomers saw in 2015. Does it look like a skull to you?

KEYWORD PROMPTS

2015 TB145 October

THE MAIN ASTEROID BELT

The largest family of asteroids lies in a zone between the orbits of Mars and Jupiter, the fourth and fifth farthest planets from the sun. This area is known as the main asteroid belt. Scientists have identified more than half a million asteroids in the main belt. But scientists believe there are billions more here.

Because there are so many asteroids, you might think that the main belt is crowded. But this neighborhood of space is anything but crowded. The 93-million-mile-thick belt is mostly empty space. If you could stand on an asteroid in the main belt, you might not be able to see your neighbor. This is because, on average, there are thousands of miles between asteroids!

TROJAN ASTEROIDS

Some asteroids travel in the same orbit as a planet. These asteroids are called Trojans. The first Trojan asteroid was discovered by astronomer Max Wolf (1863–1932). On February 22, 1906, Wolf saw an asteroid moving around Jupiter. Wolf called this asteroid Achilles. He named it after a hero in an ancient Greek myth about the Trojan War.

Achilles the asteroid shares Jupiter's orbit. Since Wolf's discovery, similar asteroids have also been called Trojans because of where they travel.

Did You Know?

If all of the asteroids in the main asteroid belt were molded into one object, it would still be smaller than Earth's moon.

Approximately 6,000 Trojans move around the sun in the same orbit as Jupiter. Jupiter's Trojans are separated into two different groups. One group of Jupiter Trojans travels in front of the planet. The second group of Trojans trails behind the planet.

Asteroid 624 Hektor is the largest known Trojan. Hektor looks like a peanut! Hektor's odd shape might be the result of a collision between two asteroids long ago. Hektor even has a tiny moon. The moon orbits Hektor every three days.

Trojan asteroids are also found moving around other planets. There is a collection of 13 known Trojans orbiting Neptune. But scientists suspect Neptune might have as many as 400 Trojans!

THEN & NOW

THEN: In 1880, Max Wolf used time-lapse photography to take pictures of asteroids. Using this method, he was able to identify more than 200 asteroids.

NOW: NASA's infrared telescope, called NEOWISE, takes pictures of the sky to help scientists find and study asteroids.

PS You can see pictures taken by NEOWISE at this website.

KEYWORD PROMPTS

NASA NEOWISE images

Neptune's Trojan asteroids are difficult to study because the planet is so far away. It is 2.7 billion miles from Earth. To give you an idea of how far that is, in 1977, NASA launched the *Voyager 2* spacecraft to study the planets farthest from the sun. This spacecraft didn't arrive in Neptune's orbit until 12 years later. That's a long flight!

Earth's Trojan is known as 2010 TK7. Canadian astronomers found TK7 after looking for Trojans for more than 15 years. Scientists have learned that TK7 is a tiny asteroid about 1,000 feet wide. The asteroid travels 50 million miles in front of Earth. Astronomers believe there could be more Earth Trojans to discover.

NEAR-EARTH ASTEROIDS

Did You Know?

The largest near-Earth asteroid to be discovered is 1036 Ganymed. It is 10 times larger than other NEAs. The asteroid is 18 miles across.

Some asteroids travel in orbits close to Earth. These asteroids are called near-Earth asteroids (NEAs). NEAs can be divided into three groups—Amor, Aten, and Apollo.

There are more than 1,600 Amor asteroids. The Amor asteroids cut across Mars's orbit. The Aten and Apollo asteroids cut across Earth's orbit. There are more than 500 known Aten asteroids and more than 3,000 Apollo asteroids.

The largest Apollo asteroid, Sisyphus, is 5 miles in diameter. In Greek mythology, Sisyphus was a man punished by the gods by having to roll a boulder up a mountain over and over again. Asteroid Sisyphus is a giant space boulder that has been orbiting the sun for millions of years. It takes Sisyphus a little more than two years to travel all the way around the sun.

DWARF PLANET

Ceres is the largest object in the asteroid belt. It's about 590 miles wide by 600 miles long. That's about the same size as Texas. An organization of professional astronomers called the International Astronomical Union decided that Ceres was a dwarf planet in 2006. Scientists think Ceres has a rocky **core** that is covered in ice and a thin, dusty crust. If this ice ever melted, Ceres would have more fresh water than Earth!

WORDS ᴛᴏ KNOW

core: the innermost layer of a planet.

Asteroids often come very close to Earth. Most small asteroids burn up in Earth's atmosphere before ever reaching the ground. According to NASA scientists, an asteroid the size of a car burns up in our atmosphere every year. And once every few million years, a really large asteroid comes close to striking Earth.

Because of this threat, astronomers are scanning the skies. They want to find Earth-crossing asteroids before they enter the atmosphere. You can read more about these asteroids in Chapter 6. In the next chapter, we'll learn about how scientists study these celestial bodies that are so far away!

 CONSIDER AND DISCUSS

It's time to consider and discuss: Why do asteroids come in many different shapes and sizes?

TROJAN ASTEROIDS

Asteroids that travel in the same orbit as a planet are called Trojans. Jupiter has Trojan asteroids. They follow Jupiter's orbit around the sun.

SUPPLIES

* ✳ old magazine covers
* ✳ pencil
* ✳ cereal bowl
* ✳ scissors
* ✳ mug
* ✳ ruler
* ✳ 2 brads
* ✳ glue stick

1 Lay the magazine cover on a flat surface. Trace around the cereal bowl and cut it out. This shape will be the sun. Repeat this step for the mug. This shape will be Jupiter.

2 Cut out a 6-by-1-inch strip of paper for your spinner.

3 Push the brad through the center of Jupiter and one end of the paper strip. Attach the other end of the strip of paper to the center of the sun with the other brad.

4 From the remaining paper, cut out two smaller strips. Trace around the glue stick twice. These shapes will stand for the Trojan asteroids orbiting the sun before and after Jupiter. Glue each Trojan to an end of one of the small strips of paper. Glue the other end of these strips to Jupiter.

5 Slowly move Jupiter around the sun. This is Jupiter's orbit. What do you notice about the Trojans?

TRY THIS! Make another circle for Earth's Trojan. Where will you place this object? Think about its orbit around the sun.

PROJECT!

THE FORCE IS WITH YOU

Gravity is a force that acts on us all the time. Earth's gravity pulls everything, including you, toward its center. On a comet such as Halley's Comet, which is shaped like a peanut, this might not happen. NASA scientists believe that Halley's gravity might pull you down and to one side as if you were in a fun house!

It isn't possible for you to take a trip to Halley's Comet, so here is an experiment that demonstrates gravity on Earth.

SUPPLIES
* science scroll
* pencil
* ruler
* 10–12 non-breakable objects, such as newspaper, tennis ball, paper clip, paper cup

1 First, test objects of different weights. Create a chart, like the one shown below, in your science scroll for this part of the experiment. Will the weight of the object affect the time it takes for the object to fall to the ground? Write down the names of the objects that you will test and your prediction beside each object.

Object	Hypothesis rank slowest–fastest (1–4)	Time	Actual rank slowest–fastest
tennis ball			
pencil			
feather			

2 Take a different object in each hand. Stand with your arms stretched out in front of you at shoulder height. Drop the objects at the same time. Write down your observations in your science scroll.

3 Repeat steps 1 and 2 for all the objects.

4 Now, drop objects that have the same weight and size. Repeat steps 1 and 2.

5 Drop objects that are the same weight, but are different sizes. Repeat steps 1 and 2.

WHAT'S HAPPENING? Objects fall because gravity pulls them down. Falling objects dropped from the same height will reach the ground at the same time, but on Earth, air resistance may cause one object to fall slower than another.

THINK ABOUT IT: The gravity on Halley's Comet is so low that it would take an object dropped from chest level two minutes to reach the ground!

WHAT TYPE OF MUSIC DO ASTEROIDS LISTEN TO?

Rock music!

ASTEROID COOKIES

Asteroids come in all shapes and sizes. Here's a way to make asteroid models that you can eat.

Caution: Ask an adult for permission, as this activity uses an oven.

1 Wash your hands. Turn on the oven to 350 degrees Fahrenheit (180 degrees Celsius). Spray the baking sheet with the non-stick spray and set to one side.

2 In the mixing bowl, combine the first five ingredients.

3 To make an asteroid cookie, take a lump of dough and press your toppings into it. You could also roll the lump of dough in these toppings. Place your asteroid cookie on the baking sheet.

4 Repeat step 3 until you have used all of the dough.

5 Place the cookies in the oven for 10 to 12 minutes. If you have made lumpier cookies, they might take longer. Once done, let the cookies cool and then enjoy.

THINK ABOUT IT: You used toppings such as candy pieces, raisins, and baking chips. What features would these represent on an asteroid?

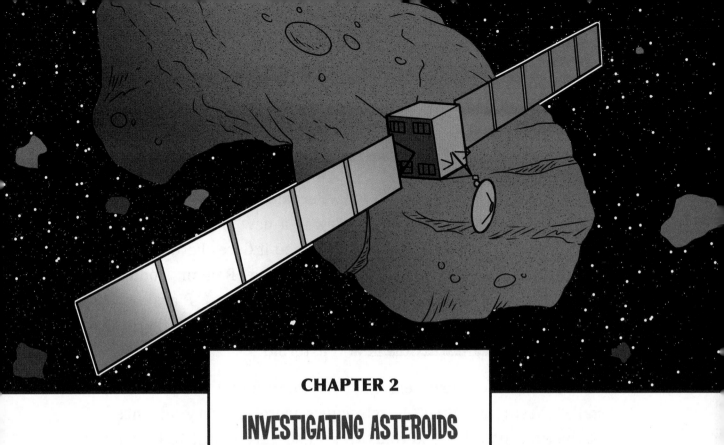

CHAPTER 2

INVESTIGATING ASTEROIDS

• • • • • • • • • • • • • • •

The solar system is filled with asteroids. But spotting asteroids from Earth can be difficult. Only the asteroid called Vesta is visible without binoculars or a telescope. This is because it is the brightest asteroid in the main asteroid belt. Even with a telescope, asteroids look like tiny specks of light. Confusing them with stars is easy. Because asteroids are so difficult to see, they were not discovered until the nineteenth century.

• •

Giuseppe Piazzi (1746–1826) was an Italian astronomer. In 1801, while working on a map of the stars, he noticed an unfamiliar object. He thought it might be a new star! But when he checked on the object a few days later, it had moved. That's strange he thought.

? **INVESTIGATE!**

Why were asteroids hard to study in the past? Why are we interested in studying them now?

Piazzi knew that stars do not wander. Stars remain in the same positions. Perhaps, thought Piazzi, it was a new small planet. He named it Ceres Ferdinandea, after the Roman goddess of agriculture. Piazzi had actually discovered the first asteroid!

Within the next few years, astronomers found the asteroids Pallas, Vesta, and Juno. As telescopes were not very advanced at the time, no other asteroids were discovered until 1845. This was when astronomers began using photography to record objects in the sky.

Astronomers developed a way to take photos of the sky during the course of several hours. This time-lapse process produced images with lots of detail. The result was a surge in new asteroid discoveries. By 1930, more than 1,000 asteroids had been discovered.

Did You Know?

In the 1800s, a new word was created to describe asteroids when astronomer William Herschel (1738-1822) wrote to poet Charles Burney Sr. for suggestions. Burney's son suggested the Greek word *asteriskos*. It became the word asteroid, meaning "star-like."

However, astronomers were not always interested in studying asteroids. This is because asteroids appeared as streaks of light in early photographs. These streaks got in the way of the objects astronomers wanted to study—stars.

Now, astronomers realize that asteroids can tell them more about the solar system. They might help people explore farther into space. They could become a source of valuable minerals. Astronomers also study asteroids to discover any that are headed our way before they cause any damage. NASA and other international space agencies have launched spacecraft and probes to gather information from asteroids.

THE FIRST CLOSE-UP

On February 17, 1996, NASA launched the *Near Earth Asteroid Rendezvous (NEAR) Shoemaker.* The mission would be the first to orbit an asteroid. Scientists wanted to study the near-Earth asteroid named 433 Eros.

IT'S HUGE!

Eros looks like someone has tugged on both of its ends. It is 20 miles long, which makes it one of the longest asteroids.

Cameras on *NEAR* took more than 160,000 photos of Eros. The photos revealed that the surface of Eros looks like a slice of Swiss cheese. It has more than 100,000 craters. Many of these craters are wider than 50 feet. Astronomers named the largest crater Psyche. If you tried to walk across Psyche, you might want to bring a bottle of water. The crater is 3 miles across.

PSYCHE, THE LARGEST CRATER ON EROS

IMAGE CREDIT: NASA

NEAR discovered many more impressive features on Eros, including a huge dent nicknamed the "saddle." The saddle divides the asteroid almost in half, creating its strange, ballet-slipper shape.

Another cool feature is its boulders. There are approximately 1 million boulders the size of a house. The largest boulder is 492 feet. That's the width of the Eiffel Tower!

At the end of the mission, NASA wanted more close-up images of Eros. It made the daring decision to land *NEAR* on the asteroid. But *NEAR* had not been designed to land. Plus, the asteroid's surface is bumpy and covered with boulders. Despite these challenges, NASA did it and *NEAR* became the first spacecraft to land on an asteroid.

ROSETTA

The European Space Agency (ESA) launched the *Rosetta* spacecraft on March 2, 2004. The spacecraft's mission was to study Comet 67P/Churyumov-Gerasimenko in the main asteroid belt. But first, the spacecraft flew by the asteroids Steins in September 2008 and Lutetia in July 2010.

What did the *Rosetta* show about these asteroids? Photos of Steins revealed it wasn't a solid rock, but a collection of loose rocks and dust stacked together like a fruit display at a grocery store. Steins is held together by weak gravity.

The sharp, angular edges of Steins reminded astronomers of a diamond. They gave craters on the asteroid gemstone names such as topaz and opal. Scientists named the largest crater on Steins, Diamond. The Diamond crater is more than 1 mile wide.

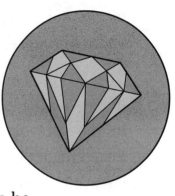

Another interesting feature on the asteroid is a set of seven pits. They look like links on a chain. Scientists are not certain how the chain was created. It may be connected to the massive impact that created the Diamond crater. The impact may have been so violent that fragments from it shattered other areas of Steins, forming the chain.

Two years later, the *Rosetta* raced past the asteroid Lutetia, traveling at 9 miles a second. The **flyby** took only a minute, but the Optical, Spectroscopic and Infrared Remote Imaging System (OSIRIS) cameras and instruments on the *Rosetta* were ready. The *Rosetta* sent maps of Lutetia's surface temperature and hundreds of images for astronomers on Earth to study.

If you could stand on Lutetia, you would see large boulders and craters, including a few more than 6 miles wide. The biggest crater on Lutetia is roughly 34 miles wide. By studying the shapes and sizes of craters, scientists can learn about the history of an asteroid. Lutetia's battered surface shows that it formed 3.9 billion years ago. This was a time when comets and asteroids crashed into planets like bumper cars.

DAWN MISSION

On September 27, 2007, NASA launched the *Dawn* mission. Scientists wanted to learn more about the history of the solar system through a study of the asteroids named Vesta and Ceres.

In 2011, *Dawn* arrived at Vesta. It is the second-largest object in the asteroid belt, after the dwarf planet Ceres. Vesta is as large as the state of Arizona. Everything on Vesta is supersized. The asteroid has a mountain twice the size of the tallest mountain on Earth, Mount Everest!

The asteroid had another surprise for astronomers. What had looked like a small dent on the asteroid's surface was, in fact, a **basin** almost as large as the asteroid! The massive basin is 285 miles across!

ASTEROID VESTA

IMAGE CREDIT: NASA/JPL-CALTECH/UCAL/MPS/DLR/IDA

In 2015, *Dawn* reached Ceres. One of the asteroid's most interesting features is a pyramid-shaped mountain. Called Ahuna Mons, the mountain is about 2.5 miles high. *Dawn* studied Ceres for more than a year, through 2016.

UNLOCKING MYSTERIES

Scientists are continuing to develop spacecraft to study asteroids. In 2016, NASA launched its first mission to take samples from an asteroid. NASA's spacecraft is called the *OSIRIS-Rex*. The craft will travel to the near-Earth asteroid Bennu by 2018.

Bennu's orbit is interesting to scientists. The asteroid's orbit brings it dangerously close to Earth every six years. Right now, Bennu is not a risk to Earth, but it could become one. As Bennu is about 1 mile around, it would cause a lot of damage if it struck Earth. This is why scientists want to collect as much information as they can on the asteroid.

NAMING ASTEROIDS

What do Mark Twain, Elvis, Beethoven, and Kleopatra have in common? They are famous figures from the past and the names of asteroids! When astronomers first encountered asteroids, they named them after figures from Greek and Roman myths. Ceres, Pallas, Juno, and Vesta were the first four asteroids discovered. They were all named after mythological characters.

EGGY MOON!

Ida is an asteroid with a moon called Dactyl. Dactyl orbits about 56 miles from Ida. While Ida's shape has been compared to a croissant, Dactyl looks more like an egg. Dactyl's rounded shape is surprising to astronomers because asteroids lack the gravity to pull their shape into a sphere.

Today, asteroids are named for cities, states, or countries, such as Acapulco, California, and Australia. Famous scientists, composers, and authors, such as Shakespeare, can also be found in space as the names of newly discovered rocky worlds. There are even asteroids named after characters from books and cartoons, including Charlie Brown and Snoopy.

WHAT DID THE SUN SAY AS THE COMET PASSED BY?

HA. HA HA HA HA

There goes a cool guy!

Scientists do not name an asteroid until its orbit can be firmly established. A newly discovered asteroid is first given a code of numbers and letters. The code shows when the asteroid was discovered.

We know that scientists have spent a lot of time finding out about asteroids! But why? What do they do with the information they learn about celestial objects far, far away? We'll find out in the next chapter!

CONSIDER AND DISCUSS

It's time to consider and discuss: Why were asteroids hard to study in the past? Why are we interested in studying them now?

ASTEROID MODEL

It wasn't always easy for astronomers to see asteroids from Earth. Asteroids often looked like specks of light before astronomers could obtain photos from spacecraft such as the *Galileo*. With an adult's permission, look at asteroid images here and create a model based on what you see.

SUPPLIES

* science scroll
* pencil
* crafting clay
* fine craft sand or tiny pebbles
* bamboo skewer, Popsicle stick

1 Write down three to five descriptive words about the asteroid you choose. Make note of any unusual features.

KEYWORD PROMPTS

NASA asteroid images

2 Take a golf-ball size of gray clay and warm it in your hands. This will make it easier to mold.

3 Mold the clay to form the basic shape of your asteroid. Look again at the image and try to make your asteroid look just like it.

4 Use your fingers, a Popsicle stick, or bamboo skewer to add details to the surface.

5 When you are happy with your model, place it to one side and let dry and harden.

THINK ABOUT IT: What do you think caused these impressions on the real asteroid's surface? Explain your answer.

REFRACTING TELESCOPE

When Giuseppe Piazzi was investigating the asteroid Ceres, he had to rely on his eyes and a simple telescope. You will not be able to study asteroids with this telescope, but you will be able to observe the stars.

Caution: Never point your telescope at the sun.

SUPPLIES

* 2 magnifying glasses or plastic lenses
* corrugated cardboard
* pencil compass
* clear tape
* 2 sheets of black craft paper

1 Place a lens over the piece of cardboard and draw a circle around it. Next, put your compass in the middle of the circle you just drew, and draw a new circle. Make the edge of your new circle ½ inch beyond your old circle.

2 Cut the cardboard along the edges of the larger circle. Then, cut out the smaller circle on the inside, leaving you with a donut shape. Repeat steps 1 and 2 for your second lens.

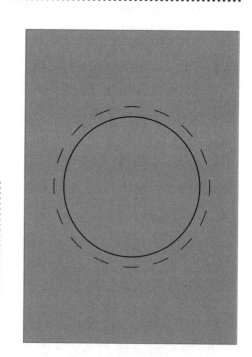

3 Roll one of your sheets into a tube about 6 inches long. The diameter of the tube should allow the cardboard you cut to fit inside snugly. Secure the tube with clear tape.

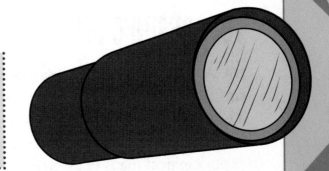

4 Take a lens and fit it into the corrugated cardboard. Then place it in the larger tube. This will be your outer telescope.

5 Insert your second lens into the inner telescope tube. Slide this tube into the larger tube, making sure the lens is facing you.

TRY THIS! Use your telescope to find the North Star. What star patterns do you notice?

THE ROSETTA STONE

The *Rosetta* spacecraft was named after the Rosetta Stone, which is a piece of rock discovered in 1799 by a French soldier near the town of Rosetta, in Egypt. This stone was special because it had the same words on it in three different languages: Greek and two ancient Egyptian languages. At the time, people knew Greek, but did not know the ancient Egyptian languages. This meant that people could translate an Egyptian language for the first time! Because of the Rosetta Stone, people could finally read lots of other Egyptian pieces and learn more about Egyptian history. Why do you think scientists named the *Rosetta* spacecraft after this special stone?

TOPOGRAPHIC MAP

NASA scientists created a map of asteroid Vesta showing surface features, such as craters. This type of map is called a topographic map. Scientists analyzed more than 17,000 images taken by *Dawn*'s cameras to create the map. Topographical maps of asteroids can be used to learn more about an asteroid's features and to determine a safe landing site for a probe. These maps use contour lines to show height. You can make a topographical map.

Caution: As this activity uses a knife, ask an adult to help.

1 Leaving the skin on, wash and dry your potato. Place the potato on a cutting board and slice off one end so that the potato stands up like a mountain.

2 Using your ruler and pen, divide the potato into four to six equal sections, around the potato. These are your contour lines!

3 Notice the contour lines and write down your observations in your science scroll.

4 Push a skewer through the potato from the top down and then remove it. This hole will help you line up the slices. Ask an adult to slice the potato into each section.

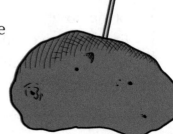

PROJECT!

5 Remove the top section and place this piece on a page in your science scroll. Trace around the piece with the pencil and set it to one side.

6 Place the second slice on the paper. Be careful to line up the hole which the skewer made. Trace around this piece and set it to one side. Repeat this step for all the remaining slices.

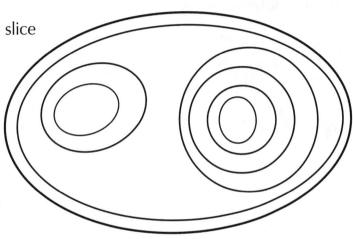

TOPOGRAPHICAL MAP EXAMPLE

7 Stack up your potato slices again and compare the potato to your topographic map.

8 What does your map look like? Write your observations down in your science scroll.

THINK ABOUT IT: Look at your map. If you had to try to land a probe on your mountain, where would you choose to land it and why? Write down your ideas in your science scroll.

ASTEROIDS AND LIGHT

Asteroids do not produce light, they reflect it. This is similar to the moon. Scientists can determine an asteroid's shape and surface features based on how the light is reflected. You can see how asteroids reflect light using a potato.

SUPPLIES

* science scroll
* pencil
* bamboo skewers
* 3 to 4 baking potatoes
* desk lamp

1 Write your prediction down in your science scroll. How do you think the shapes of the potatoes will affect how the light is reflected?

2 Push a bamboo skewer through one of your potatoes. If a single skewer cannot support the weight of your potato, use two.

3 Turn on your desk light and put out the room light. Hold the potato near the light and rotate it slowly. Take your time. Observe how the light falls on each feature. Write your observations down in your science scroll. Try your other potatoes. How are they different?

TRY THIS! Do you think rotating the potatoes horizontally will change your results? Make a prediction and test it out.

THEN & NOW

THEN: On June 30, 1908, the largest asteroid in recent history exploded above Russia.

NOW: Each year, Asteroid Day is celebrated on June 30. This is an annual event to raise awareness about the risk of asteroid impacts.

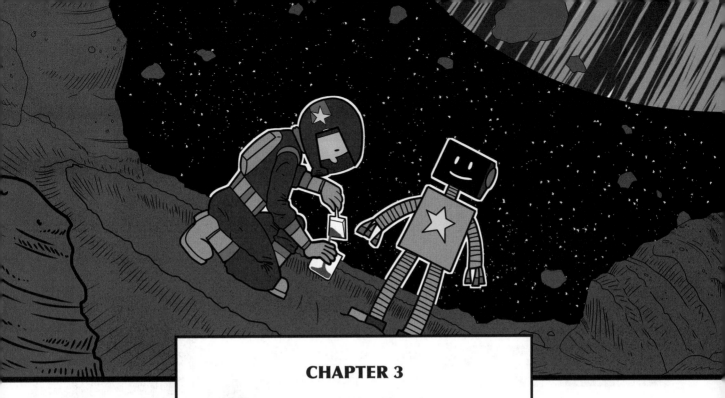

CHAPTER 3

MINERALS, MINING, AND ASTEROIDS

Look around you. What colors do you see in the world?
Did you know that space has color, too? Some asteroids
have a red tint, and others shine brightly like metal. Many
are black or brown. To astronomers, asteroid colors are
clues. Color can reveal what an asteroid is made of.

Each **mineral** on an asteroid's surface reflects light differently.
The amount of light an asteroid reflects is called **spectra**. There
are three main spectral classes in the asteroid belt. They are
carbonaceous (C), stony (S),
and metal-rich (M).

? INVESTIGATE!

How can asteroids be
useful to people on Earth?

WORDS TO KNOW

mineral: a naturally occurring
solid found in rocks and in the
ground. Rocks are made of
minerals. Gold and diamonds
are precious minerals.

spectra: bands of colors that
a ray of light can be separated
into. Singular is spectrum.

carbon: an element found in living things, including plants. Carbon is also found in diamonds, charcoal, and graphite.

element: a pure substance that cannot be broken down into a simpler substance. Everything in the universe is made up of combinations of elements. Oxygen and gold are two elements.

WORDS ⊕ KNOW

CARBONACEOUS ASTEROIDS

The largest group of asteroids are C-type asteroids. They are made of **carbon**, which is one of the most important **elements**. Pencils, plastics, and the charcoal your parents might use in a grill contain carbon. Carbon makes asteroids appear so dark that they are almost black. C-type asteroids are some of the oldest asteroids. These are found in the outer asteroid belt.

Asteroid Mathilde is a C-type asteroid. Mathilde is twice as far from Earth as Earth is from the sun! This asteroid has lots of craters and its surface is as dark as an asphalt playground. If reflects only about 4 percent of the sun's light.

MATHILDE
IMAGE CREDIT: NASA

STONY ASTEROIDS

S-type, or stony asteroids, are made of round lumps of rocks and clay. Some S-types are rich in metals such as iron, nickel, and cobalt. These make them a light-gray color. Stony asteroids are found in the inner asteroid belt.

lava: hot, melted rock that has risen to the surface.

WORDS ⑩ KNOW

The asteroid Gaspra is an example of a stony asteroid. Gaspra was discovered in 1916. The asteroid became better known after the *Galileo* spacecraft flew passed it on October 29, 1991. Gaspra's surface is covered with rocks and more than 600 small craters.

Two years later, *Galileo* whizzed past another S-type asteroid, Ida. Ida's surface is covered with hundreds of craters and dozens of massive boulders. The largest boulder is a fourth the width of the entire asteroid.

Did You Know?

In 1993, *Galileo* discovered the first binary asteroid, 243. Binary asteroids have two parts that orbit each other. Scientists believe that 16 percent of all near-Earth asteroids are binary. There are even asteroids with two moons. They are called triple systems.

METALLIC ASTEROIDS

M-types, or metallic asteroids, are mostly made of metals such as nickel and iron. They are found in the middle of the asteroid belt. Their high metal content makes them much brighter than C-type or S-type asteroids.

The asteroid Vesta is an M-type asteroid. Based on data from the *Dawn* spacecraft, astronomers believe that lava once flowed over Vesta.

WHAT BOOKS DO COMETS READ?

HA HA HA HA HA

Comet books!

Vesta's crust is now covered with basaltic rock, which forms after lava cools and hardens. When the lava bubbled to the asteroid's surface, blobs of heavier materials such as iron sank. They formed Vesta's metallic core.

MINING ASTEROIDS

Asteroids have many valuable **resources**. Some contain gold, platinum, and iron. They also include rare earth metals. These metals are used in lasers, cancer treatment drugs, cameras, and telescope lenses.

Only a few companies and governments are investigating the mining of asteroids. This is because mining asteroids for their resources presents several problems. Space missions cost a lot of money. It can take billions of dollars to build a spacecraft. It takes more money to launch it. Many people still think it's possible to **mine** asteroids for metals, and they're working on solutions to these challenges.

A company called Planetary Resources believes that people will one day mine in space. Planetary Resources has to figure out how to build low-cost mining spacecraft. One idea is to build spacecraft on an assembly line just like cars are made.

Did You Know?

In the future, there might be an asteroid miner that looks like a snow blower. Instead of blowing snow, the spinning blade would propel rubble into an extra-heavy plastic bag.

GLUG, GLUG

Asteroids might even have water on them or below the surface. Right now, astronauts have to bring and recycle all the water they need for a trip into space. If they could get water from asteroids, they might be able to travel even farther into space! Scientists are working on the challenge of getting water from asteroids in the hopes of making long-term life in space possible.

COLLECTING ASTEROID SAMPLES

Before space mining can begin, asteroid resources have to be studied. Japan's *Hayabusa* probe was the first to collect samples from an asteroid. The probe's name means "falcon" in Japanese.

The Japan Aerospace Exploration Agency (JAXA) launched *Hayabusa* on May 8, 2003, and sent it to the near-Earth asteroid Itokawa. The probe was equipped with three cameras and a near-infrared spectrometer (NIS). Astronomers use spectrometers to study minerals on the surfaces of asteroids.

For several months, *Hayabusa* mapped and photographed the peanut-shaped asteroid. In November 2005, *Hayabusa* became the first probe to collect asteroid samples. After bouncing twice off the surface, it successfully collected more than 1,500 dust grains by firing small metal balls to loosen the asteroid's surface. The dust was collected in canisters, and the probe returned to Earth in 2010. Success!

? **CONSIDER AND DISCUSS**

It's time to consider and discuss: How can asteroids be useful to people on Earth?

THEN & NOW

THEN: On December 22, 1891, Max West took the first photo of an asteroid, called 323 Brucia.

- -

NOW: *Lucy* is the name of a new NASA space mission that will send a probe to study asteroids near Jupiter in 2021.

PROJECT!

UNDERSTANDING COLOR

Astronomers use color to estimate what an asteroid is made of. Each mineral or metal has a particular color. In this activity, you are going to experiment with a **prism** to see if you can see the light spectrum.

SUPPLIES

* science scroll
* pencil
* small measuring cup
* roasting pan
* small mirror
* sheet of white paper

1 In your scroll, predict what you think is going to happen when light passes through a prism and why. Write out the steps to the experiment.

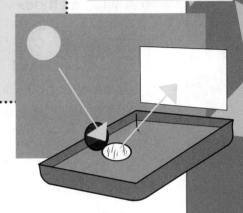

2 Place your roasting pan on a flat surface in a sunny room. Pour about 2 cups of water into your roasting pan. It should be about two-thirds full.

3 Take your small mirror and hold it under the water, facing the sun. Hold the paper with your other hand. Angle the paper and the mirror until the light shines on the paper.

4 Observe the spectrum. Write down your observations in your science scroll. Look at your prediction. Do your results reflect your prediction? Why or why not?

WHAT'S HAPPENING? The mirror in your experiment acts like a prism. It splits the light. Each color has a different wavelength. On one end of the spectrum is violet. Violet bends more than any other color. The color red bends the least.

WORDS TO KNOW

prism: an object that disperses light and reflects it into the full color range of the rainbow.

43

ASTEROID SAMPLES

SUPPLIES

* foil roasting pan or plastic container
* sand
* water
* pebbles
* measuring cup
* science scroll
* pencil

Landing on an asteroid is no piece of cake! But touching down on the surface isn't the end of the journey. Just as it can take many tries to score a goal, the *Hayabusa* tried several times to get samples from asteroid Itokawa. In this experiment, you are going to test what methods work best for retrieving samples.

1 Fill about 1 inch of your foil tray with sand. Pour water gently across the sand. Don't add more than your sand can absorb. This will be your asteroid surface.

2 Let your new asteroid dry for 24 hours, until the surface of the sand has hardened.

3 Now collect space rock samples! Bring your tray outside, and try to loosen the asteroid's surface by throwing pebbles at it.

4 Remove the pebbles from the tray. Now, gently tilt to pour your loosened sample into the measuring cup. Make sure you don't let the hardened asteroid fall out.

5 Write down the size of your sample in your science scroll.

6 Now, try using items of different shapes to loosen the surface. Which shape will work best? Make a prediction and test it out. Keep measuring the amount of sample you collect and put this information in a bar graph.

PROJECT!

ASTEROID MINER

Just as the California Gold Rush encouraged people to rush West to discover gold between 1848 and 1855, space mining might encourage people to rush into space! This project will let you design an asteroid miner.

SUPPLIES

* small box
* masking tape
* paper clips
* rubber bands
* plastic bottle caps or cardboard
* 4 long bamboo skewers
* clay
* drinking straw
* balloon

1 Answer the following questions. How is your mining vehicle going to move over the surface of the asteroid? How is it going to mine the asteroid? How is it going to collect what it mines? Will your miner work independently or will it need a person to control it?

2 Look at your supplies and decide which piece will be the body of the miner.

3 Work on your wheels. You can cut cardboard into circles or use bottle caps. The bamboo skewers can connect the wheels. Think about how your wheels will rotate. You can use the clay to stop your wheels from falling off the skewers.

4 The balloon and straw can be used to create motion. Think about where you will have to place the straw. Then blow up the balloon and slide it onto the straw and let go.

TRY THIS! Did larger or smaller wheels change your results? After making a prediction, test it out.

45

CHAPTER 4

CURIOUS ABOUT COMETS

• • • • • • • • • • • • • •

**Long ago, ancient astronomers noticed something
curious. Shiny new lights sometimes lit up the evening
sky. But these lights did not behave like stars. They
seemed to come out of nowhere. The objects moved
slowly across the sky for a few days or weeks. Then, they
disappeared just as quickly as they had appeared.**

• •

Astronomers described these objects
as stars with tails. Others said they
were flaming swords or fiery torches.
What were these mysterious moving
lights? They were comets!

 INVESTIGATE!

Why did people fear comets
in the past? Why aren't most
people afraid of them now?

Many people feared comets. Some believed they were evil spirits. As it was not yet possible to study space with binoculars or telescopes, different cultures made up stories to explain what they saw. Many of these stories about comets were full of fear.

People blamed comets for natural disasters, wars, and death. The last ruler of the Aztecs, Montezuma II, is said to have seen a comet. When he asked his priests to tell him what it meant, they predicted that his kingdom would disappear.

culture: the beliefs and way of life of a group of people, which can include religion, language, art, clothing, food, holidays, and more.

coincidence: a remarkable timing of events or circumstances without an apparent connection.

foretold: predicted.

philosopher: a person who thinks about and questions the way things are in the world and in the universe.

WORDS TO KNOW

Soon after, in 1519, the Spanish landed in Mexico. Within five years, Montezuma II was dead and his once massive empire had fallen to the Spanish. This was just a coincidence, but it was seen as proof that comets foretold the future.

COMET SCIENCE

Scientists longed to understand comets. One of the first people to study comets was Aristotle (384–322 BCE) a great Greek philosopher and scientist.

nucleus: the center of a comet. Plural is nuclei.

coma: an envelope of gases around a comet's nucleus.

geyser: a spring of water that, when heated, bursts into the air.

WORDS ⊕ KNOW

Aristotle thought that the sun heated Earth's surface. He reasoned that this heat rose into the air, where it occasionally caught fire, creating a comet. Today, we know that Aristotle's explanation of comets is not correct. But many people believed his ideas for centuries.

Much later, English astronomer Edmond Halley (1656–1742) wanted to solve the mystery about comets. Halley did not think there was a link between comets and Earth's surface. He believed that comets were bodies in space. Halley set out to use numbers to explain his theory.

WHAT ARE COMETS?

Comets are chunks of water, ice, rock, and dust. They zip along through space and come in all shapes and sizes. Some are no larger than a boulder. Others are the size of Manhattan! Comets have three main parts, the **nucleus**, the **coma**, and the tail.

The center of a comet is called its nucleus. Scientists have been able to measure the nuclei of 10 different comets. Most are less than 6 miles across. A few comets have massive nuclei measuring more than 20 miles wide, even up to 125 miles wide.

Some nuclei are rough and rocky. They have steep pits and huge, mountain-like structures. Parts of their surface may be smooth or covered with small holes. Jets of gas and dust burst from these holes like water erupting from a **geyser**.

WORDS TO KNOW

Halley's friend, Isaac Newton (1643–1727), was a mathematician. Newton had written about the movement of comets. Halley used Newton's ideas to figure out the orbit of one comet.

First, Halley studied people's observations of comets from 1337 to 1698. He noticed there had been comet sightings in 1531, 1607, and 1682—exactly 76 years apart! Halley decided that it must be the same comet. He predicted that the comet would return in 1758.

Halley did not live to see his prediction come true, but he was right. Comets are objects in space that move in orbits around the sun. The returning comet was named after him.

HERE COMES THE SUN

A comet's nucleus remains frozen until the comet approaches the sun. As the sun's heat warms the nucleus, the frozen water does not melt. It changes into gas. This process is called sublimation.

Gas and dust shoot out of holes in the crust to form a cloud around the nucleus. This cloud is called a coma. From Earth, the coma looks like a fuzzy halo. Comas can grow to be as big as the sun, which is 864,938 miles across. Almost 1 million planet Earths could fit inside the sun!

Some comets form a tail, but not all of them do. Tails sweep away from the sun, making the comet look like it has hair. This is what led ancient Greek sky watchers to call comets *kometes*, Greek for "hairy stars."

Comet tails can have two parts. The dust tail is made of grains of dust. The particles are released from the comet's icy nucleus as the hot sun bakes the comet's surface. They glow yellow because they reflect sunlight.

Dust tails can be more than 1 million miles long! A tail this size could wrap around our Earth more than 40 times!

Did You Know?

Comets that fly very close to the sun are called sungrazers. Sometimes, their orbits take them within a few thousand miles of the sun's surface. Most sungrazers don't survive this close encounter. They are quickly torn to pieces.

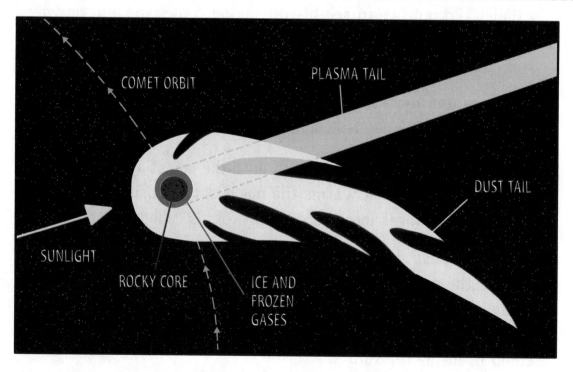

COMET ORBIT

PLASMA TAIL

DUST TAIL

SUNLIGHT

ROCKY CORE

ICE AND FROZEN GASES

A second, thinner tail, is made of gas. It is called an ion or plasma tail. Plasma is hot, glowing gas. When the plasma is heated, it appears blue. The plasma tail is pushed away from the nucleus by the solar wind. As the comet nears the sun, the tail grows.

A GREAT ADVENTURE

In 2014, the *Rosetta* orbiter reached Comet 67P/Churyumov-Gerasimenko. It had taken *Rosetta* 10 years to reach the comet. On board the spacecraft was a small lander called Philae. Scientists at the European Space Agency (ESA) hoped Philae would land on the comet's nucleus. No other probe had ever landed on a comet before.

To prepare for the landing, the *Rosetta* flew past Comet 67P, gathering more information. The comet's nucleus is only 2.5 miles wide. Scientists were worried when they saw pictures of the comet. They believed it would look like a ball. Instead, it looks like a rubber ducky with bumps, boulders, and cliffs!

HOW IS A COMET LIKE A LIZARD?

They both have tails.

THEN & NOW

THEN: Comets were so mysterious they frightened people.

NOW: People know that comets are icy leftovers from the earliest days of the solar system.

On November 12, 2014, scientists waited as Philae began its descent. Because 67P's gravity is so weak, the lander fell slowly. After seven hours, scientists received a signal. It was time to cheer! After bouncing twice, Philae had touched down safely! For nearly 60 hours, Philae surveyed the surface. The probe then fell asleep because it did not have enough sunlight to keep running.

Scientists discovered the nucleus of Comet 67P is not a solid lump of rock as they had thought. It is a fluffy ball made of ice, dust, and organic materials. Comet 67P is so light that it could float on water!

Two years later, the *Rosetta* made another exciting discovery. It found important molecules on the comet. The spacecraft detected water, carbon monoxide, and carbon dioxide. But 67P's water molecules are different from water found on Earth. They have a different type of hydrogen. This information on water helped scientists to understand that asteroids, not comets, likely brought water to Earth. We'll learn more about comets in the next chapter.

? CONSIDER AND DISCUSS

It's time to consider and discuss: Why did people fear comets in the past? Why aren't most people afraid of them now?

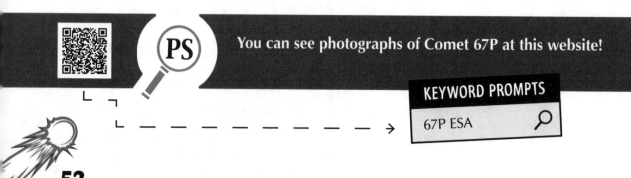

PS You can see photographs of Comet 67P at this website!

KEYWORD PROMPTS

67P ESA

EXPLORING COMET ORBITS

SUPPLIES

✳ cardboard, 24 by 24 inches
✳ 2 pushpins
✳ dental floss
✳ sharp pencil

Comets orbit the sun in elliptical paths, not circles. In this activity, you are going to make an ellipse.

1 Put a pushpin in the center of your cardboard.

2 Tear off about a ruler's length of floss and tie the ends together. Loop the floss around the pushpin. Put the tip of the pencil in the loop and pull gently. Now draw a line around the pushpin keeping the floss taut. You should have a circle.

3 To draw an ellipse, put two pushpins into the cardboard near the center, about 4 inches apart. Put your floss loop around both pins.

4 Put the tip of the pencil in the loop and pull gently until the loop looks like a triangle. Now draw a line around the pushpins keeping the floss taut until an ellipse forms. Compare the circle to the ellipse— how do they differ?

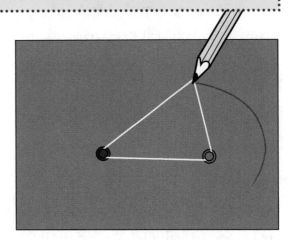

TRY THIS! Mark the position of the sun on your cardboard. Think about an asteroid's orbit around the sun. Try placing the pins at different distances and using different lengths of floss to create different orbits.

WORDS TO KNOW

elliptical: shaped like an ellipse, or an oval.

MAKE YOUR OWN COMET

Comets are made of water, ice, dust, and gases. They come in many different sizes and shapes. In this activity, you are going to make your own comets.

Caution: An adult needs to help you with the blender.

1 Ask an adult to crush ice cubes in a blender. You will need about 4 to 6 cups of crushed ice. Pour the ice into a large mixing bowl.

2 Scoop some of the ice onto the plastic tray. Add some sand with the spoon. Put on the gloves and mix the ice and sand together. You will need to work quickly so the ice doesn't melt!

3 Scoop the sand and ice mixture into your containers. Only fill the containers three-quarters full. Pour a little water on top of the sand and ice mixture.

Did You Know? Astronomers have recorded strange sounds from coming from Comet 67P. Its song sounds like a series of clicks. Scientists believe that the singing is vibrations in the comet's magnetic field.

4 Place the containers in a freezer for a couple of hours or until they are solid.

WORDS TO KNOW

magnetic: having the properties of a magnet, capable of attracting metal.

PROJECT!

5 Run a little warm water over the container to loosen your comets. Turn them upside down on the baking sheet and tap a few times to release.

6 Place the tray with the comets somewhere you can observe them all day. Write your observations down in your science scroll. Look at the indents on your comets. On a real comet, jets of gas would escape from these holes. After the ice has melted, what are you left with?

WHAT'S HAPPENING? After years and years of traveling around the sun, comets eventually lose so much material that they disintegrate into gas, dust, and pebbles.

COMET LOVEJOY

An amateur astronomer named Terry Lovejoy discovered a new comet on December 2, 2011. Named Comet Lovejoy after its discoverer, this sungrazer surprised astronomers later that month by surviving its brush with the sun.

COMET LOVEJOY
IMAGE CREDIT: NASA

  You can see video of the comet's close encounter with the sun here.

KEYWORD PROMPTS

comet Lovejoy NASA

EXPERIMENT WITH LANDERS

Have you ever given someone a piggyback? This is how the _Rosetta_ carried the lander Philae into space. Once the _Rosetta_ was in position, it released Philae. The probe's three legs unfolded to prepare for descent. Can you design a lander that does not fall over on impact?

SUPPLIES

* science scroll
* pencil
* cardboard
* rubber bands
* straws
* postcard-sized magazine advertisements
* small marshmallows
* scissors
* tape

1 Write down goals for your lander in your science scroll. You need to build a lander that does not fall over or break on impact. What will you use to cushion the landing? Look at the materials you have gathered and write down ideas.

2 Use the cardboard as your lander's base. Be creative. How will you use the straws and elastic bands?

3 Try folding the magazine advertisements accordion style to create springs. You can also add materials such as marshmallows to ease the landing.

4 Test your lander. Drop from chest-height and write down your results. Does it bounce? Does it tip over?

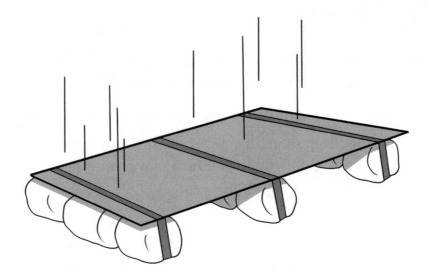

5 Organize your results into a chart. How does the lander work when dropped from different heights?

TRY THIS! Would dropping your lander onto different surfaces, such as pebbles, macaroni pieces, or flour, change your results? Would it change your design? Make a prediction, test it out, and redesign your lander.

Did You Know?

While the *Rosetta* is now about 251 million miles from Earth at Comet 67P, it had to travel about 4 billion miles to get to the comet because it had to move around and around to catch the comet in orbit!

SUPPLIES
* friends to play

CREATE A MYTH

Myths about comets come from all over the world. In this game, you are going to create a comet myth with a group of friends.

1 Ask your friends to sit in a circle. The first player says the opening sentence of the myth. The next player must repeat this sentence and add a new sentence.

2 Go around the circle with each player reciting the previous sentences and adding a new sentence to the story. Continue playing until everyone has had a turn.

3 To make the game challenging, players must add a sentence in alphabetical order. The first player's sentence begins with the letter A. For example: "A bright light lit up the sky last night." The next player must create a sentence that begins with the letter B and so on. In this version of the game, it is not necessary to repeat back the previous player's line.

TRY THIS! Have someone write down your myth as you go. At the end you'll have a story that you can illustrate. Create your own book and read your story aloud.

CHAPTER 5

COOL COMETS

• • • • • • • • • • • • • • • • • • • •

Imagine you're heading to school. After lacing up your shoes and opening up the front door, which way will you go? You probably walk the same path to school and home every day. Just like you, comets and asteroids also have paths that they follow again and again. But unlike your walk to school and back, a comet's orbit can take hundreds of years!

• • • • • • • • • • • • • • • • • • • •

Comets move in long, elliptical orbits around the sun. The oval shape of their orbits bring them closer to the sun for part of their orbits.

? INVESTIGATE!

Why do we study objects that we might not be able to see within our lifetime?

short-period comet: a comet that takes less than 200 years to travel around the sun.

long-period comet: a comet that takes more than 200 years to travel around the sun.

WORDS ⊙ KNOW

After rounding the sun, comets move farther and farther away. This is why we can see them for just part of their orbit.

Astronomers place comets in one of two categories, depending on their orbits. Comets with orbits of less than 200 years are called **short-period comets**. Comets with orbits greater than 200 years are **long-period comets**.

Some long-period comets take thousands or even millions of years to orbit the sun. Comet Hale-Bopp is a long-period comet that won't be seen from earth for another 2,000 years! It's about the same age as our sun—4.5 billion years old.

Comet Kohoutek is another long-term comet. It takes 75,000 years to orbit the sun and was last visible from Earth in 1973. What do you think Earth will look like when Kohoutek comes again?

MOST-WATCHED COMET

In 1995, two separate sky watchers discovered Hale-Bopp while it was still more than 665 million miles away from the sun. Comets this far away usually appear as a dot, but not Comet Hale-Bopp. It was incredibly bright. From May 1996 to November 1997, Hale-Bopp lit up the skies above Earth. Because it was so bright, sky watchers could see the comet without using binoculars or telescopes. This is how the Hale-Bopp comet became the most-watched comet in history.

THE OORT CLOUD

The **Oort Cloud** is not like a cloud you might see from your window. It's a cloud that surrounds our entire solar system and is filled with ice, dust grains, and gases. Scientists think it is home to long-period comets that orbit the sun beyond Pluto, which is about 4 to 6 billion miles from Earth.

Oort Cloud: a collection of comets and icy material on the fringes of our solar system. It is theorized that long-period comets come from the Oort Cloud.

astronomical unit (AU): a unit of measure used in space. One AU is the average distance from the earth to the sun, 93 million miles.

WORDS TO KNOW

Did You Know?

The longest-period comet is called Delavan. Delavan was last seen in 1914 and won't be coming back for a visit for another 24 million years!

The cloud is named after Dutch astronomer Jan Oort (1900–1990). Oort studied comets in the 1950s and is one of greatest astronomers of the twentieth century.

Oort noticed things about long-period comets. He saw that they fall into the inner solar system from different directions. He also noticed that the farthest point of their orbits is 50,000 **astronomical units (AU)** from the sun. Oort predicted that long-period comets come from a region of space just outside the solar system.

WHAT DID THE DADDY COMET SAY TO THE BABY COMET?

HA HA HA HA HA

You are a chip off the old block!

Kuiper belt: a region of icy bodies beyond Neptune's orbit that includes Pluto and Eris. It is theorized that short period comets come from the Kuiper belt.

WORDS ⑳ KNOW

Astronomers believe there might be trillions of comets in the Oort Cloud. As the cloud is so far away from Earth, no one knows for sure what's in it. One day, people might know this answer because of NASA's *Voyager I* spacecraft.

NASA launched the *Voyager 1* spacecraft in 1977 to study the far solar system. The spacecraft is not expected to reach the Oort Cloud for another 300 years! According to NASA, it will take *Voyager 1* another 14,000 to 28,000 years to exit the cloud. That is how large the Oort cloud is.

Did You Know?

In the future, comets could become the travel centers of space. Comet nuclei contain water and dust rich in minerals. Space travelers might refuel their spacecraft, grab a drink of water, and even get a bite to eat on comets!

THE KUIPER BELT

The Kuiper belt is a cold region of space. It's not possible to see the Kuiper Belt from Earth because it is on the far edge of our solar system, beyond Neptune. It is about 3 billion miles from the sun. The Kuiper belt is named for a Dutch-American astronomer, Gerard Kuiper (1905–1973). In 1951, Kuiper wanted to know why some comets visit our solar system every few dozen years while others take far longer.

Kuiper suggested that there is another flat ring with comets beyond Neptune's orbit. He believed comets that take less than 200 years to orbit the sun come from this area.

For decades, astronomers didn't have the right tools to prove if the Kuiper belt was real or not. It wasn't until 1992 that the first Kuiper belt object was discovered. This was when astronomers Dave Jewitt (1958–) and Jane Luu (1963–) spied a dot of light beyond Neptune. The discovery proved that Kuiper's theory was correct.

As the Kuiper belt is so far away, objects within the belt appear faint from Earth. But with the space-based Hubble Space Telescope, scientists can see objects in the Kuiper belt more clearly.

THEN & NOW

THEN: The Hubble Space Telescope provides scientists with images of the Kuiper belt.

NOW: After its launch in 2018, the James Webb Space Telescope will be the most powerful telescope in history.

63

NEW HORIZONS

In 2015, the *New Horizons* spacecraft became the first mission to explore the Kuiper belt. After studying Pluto, scientists put the spacecraft on a course for a comet 1 billion miles beyond Pluto. This icy world is called 2014 MU69. The comet is thought to be 30 miles across, about only 1 percent the size of Pluto. The comet is significant because it has remained frozen for billions of years. It might be able to tell astronomers what our solar system was like when it was very young. *New Horizons* is not expected to reach the comet until 2019.

You can see some of the objects in the Kuiper belt at this website.

KEYWORD PROMPTS

Kuiper Hubble

Since Jewitt and Luu's discovery, more than 1,000 Kuiper belt objects have been identified. However, astronomers believe that there may be hundreds of millions of objects in the belt, including short-period comets. Most of the known Kuiper belt objects are small. On average, they are between 6 and 31 miles across. The dwarf planets Pluto and Eris are the largest objects in the Kuiper belt. They are both roughly 1,400 miles across.

Comets are super interesting to learn about. But what can these flying celestial objects tell us about our own planet? Find out in the next chapter!

CONSIDER AND DISCUSS

It's time to consider and discuss: Why do we study objects that we might not be able to see within our lifetime?

TIME TRAVEL

The Kuiper belt is so far from Earth that it takes today's spacecraft more than 10 years to get there. A lot of things can change in 10 years. In this activity, you are going to create a chart showing what you think your life will be like in 10 years.

1 In your science scroll, create a chart with two columns. At the top of one column write, "My Life Now" and in the second column write, "My Life in 10 Years."

2 Draw a picture of yourself now and in the future.

3 Write down what grade you are in and what you currently do after school. What are your favorite foods, books, and movies? Think about what you might enjoy when you are older and write down your ideas.

4 Describe where you live. Include information on your city or town, home, and family. Where will you be living in the future?

5 You will have to keep your science scroll safe for the next 10 years. Will your predictions turn out to be true?

TRY THIS! Draw or take pictures of objects in your town, home, school, or room. Include these images in your chart.

PROJECT!

SOLAR WIND

What happens when a comet nears the sun and the comet's nucleus warms up? Where do the gas and dust go? Invite a friend to discover the answer with you in this experiment. Be sure to do this experiment in a large room.

> **Caution:** Ask an adult for permission before using the hairdryer. The hairdryer can become hot, so be careful.

1 Make the comet's orbit on a carpet. This activity is best done with a friend. You first need to create two foci. Lay the yardstick on the carpet and make a chalk mark at one end. Before making the second focus point, know that the distance between the foci will determine the size of your ellipse. You can experiment with this second measurement.

2 Cut a piece of twine at least twice as long as the distance between the foci.

3 Tape the ends of the twine down to either point. Now, pull the twine out taut with your chalk.

SUPPLIES

* yardstick or ruler
* sidewalk chalk
* twine
* masking tape
* newsprint
* tissue paper or streamers
* sharp pencil
* sharpie
* hairdryer
* extension cord
* science scroll
* pencil

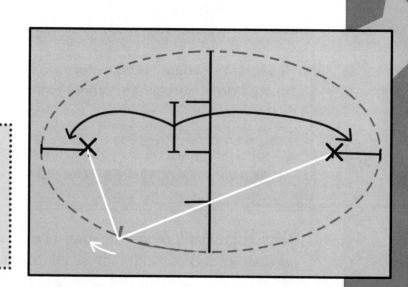

PROJECT!

4 Keep the string straight as you slowly draw your ellipse. You can see an example at this website.

KEYWORD PROMPTS

draw an ellipse 🔍

5 Scrunch up a few sheets of newsprint to make a ball. Take your sharpie and make a small mark on the ball. This mark will designate the front of your comet.

6 Use about four 12-inch streamers or cut the tissue paper into streamers and tape to the back of your comet.

7 Push the sharp end of the pencil into the bottom of your comet. You may need to tape it into place.

8 Plug the hairdryer into a wall socket or an extension cord. Have a friend hold the hairdryer facing the ellipse. This person will be the sun. The hairdryer is the solar wind. Keep the hairdryer on a low-heat or cool setting.

9 Hold your comet in front of you and walk slowly around the ellipse. You may walk in either direction—few comets orbit the sun in a clockwise direction.

10 When you are done, write your observations and draw a picture in your science scroll.

TRY THIS! Do you think a comet's shape would change your results? Form a hypothesis and test it out!

WRITE SPACE TWEETS

The *New Horizon's* probe is flying toward Comet 2014 MU69. No one knows yet what the comet will be like. Create a pretend Twitter account to inform the world about the project!

1 Tweets have 140 characters or less, but for this activity use short, complete sentences.

2 Imagine that you are part of this exciting trip. You need to post on Twitter about your voyage, your landing, and this icy object.

3 In a series of eight to ten imaginary tweets, describe the comet's surface. Notice if there are any features, such as craters or boulders.

COMET 2014 MU69 HAS NO ATMOSPHERE, BUT PLENTY OF GOOD VIBES!

4 Will these features provide you with clues about what is below the surface? What else do you observe about the comet?

TRY THIS! Create a pretend Instagram account for your comet. Draw pictures of what you might post to your comet's Instagram. Create a song and a flag for your comet.

CHAPTER 6

MYSTERIOUS METEORS

A streak of light flashes across the sky. A window shatters. Two kids pick up a strange-looking black rock in their backyard. What do these events have in common? They all began with a piece of space rock. You might call it a shooting star. Astronomers call these glowing trails of light meteors.

Space is full of rocky debris from when the universe first formed. A meteoroid is a piece of rocky or metallic material from asteroids or comets journeying through space. Like a comet or asteroid, a meteoroid orbits the sun. Sometimes, a meteoroid is pulled into Earth's atmosphere by the planet's strong gravity.

WORDS TO KNOW

meteor: the streak of light when a bit of rock or dust enters Earth's atmosphere.

meteoroid: a rock that orbits the sun. It is smaller than an asteroid and at least as large as a speck of dust.

INVESTIGATE!

What can ancient craters tell us about the history of Earth?

When a meteoroid enters Earth's atmosphere, astronomers call it a meteor. As the meteor falls, it collides with air molecules in Earth's atmosphere. These collisions slow the meteor down and create friction.

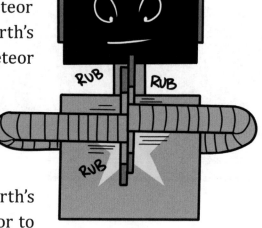

An example of friction is when you rub two objects, such as your hands, together. What happens if you rub your hands together quickly? Friction in Earth's atmosphere causes the surface of a meteor to heat up, too. Eventually, the meteor gets so hot that it bursts into flames. As it burns, it leaves a trail of light in the sky. This is why people call meteors falling or shooting stars. The trail of light lasts for only a short time because the meteor burns up completely.

Most meteors are no larger than dust grains. Each year, thousands of tons of space dust rain down on Earth.

Did You Know?

The words *meteoroid, meteor,* and *meteorite* all come from the Greek word *meteoron,* meaning "thing in the heaven above." A meteoroid is a rock that orbits the sun. If a meteoroid or a piece of rock or dust from an asteroid or comet enters Earth's atmosphere, it's a meteor. If the piece of rock survives it's trip through the atmosphere and lands on Earth, it's a meteorite.

When larger meteors enter Earth's atmosphere, they burn brighter and longer. Known as fireballs, they make a crackling sound like logs on fire.

meteorite: a piece of space rock that falls to Earth.

WORDS TO KNOW

Fireballs come in many colors—green, yellow, orange, red, and white. Their color depends on the gases surrounding the meteoroid. In 1974, a fireball thousands of times brighter than a full moon appeared above western Czechoslovakia. It holds the record for the brightest fireball photographed.

Sometimes, fireballs explode near the end of their descent. these are called bolides, a word that in ancient Greek meant "flaming spear." When a meteor strikes Earth's surface, it is called a meteorite.

TWENTIETH-CENTURY STRIKE

On June 30, 1908, a fireball blazed across the sky above the Stony Tunguska River in Siberia, Russia. It was followed by an ear-splitting sound as the object exploded. The explosion could be heard more than 600 miles away. Hundreds of miles from the explosion, the ground shook, knocking people over. Closer to the blast, trees were knocked down like dominoes.

Scientists are still not sure what caused the damage. Some scientists believe that an asteroid exploded in the air. Other scientists believe that a piece of a comet exploded above the ground. For several days afterward, the nighttime sky glowed so brightly that it could be seen 3,000 miles away, in Great Britain. The light might have been caused by dust grains from the comet reflecting the light.

WORDS ᴛᴏ KNOW

meteor shower: when many pieces of dust burn up in Earth's atmosphere.

constellation: a group of stars in the sky that resembles a certain shape, such as the Big Dipper.

Northern Hemisphere: the half of Earth north of the equator.

WORDS ᴛᴏ KNOW

METEOR SHOWER

What happens when pieces of a comet are blown off by the sun's solar winds? That's when the night sky puts on a spectacular light show! On these particular nights, you might see many meteors falling. Astronomers call these many sparks of light a **meteor shower**.

When a comet enters the inner solar system, the sun warms the comet's surface. Dust and ice are then loosened from the comet's surface. The comet moves on, but these dust grains are left behind. When Earth crosses this dusty trail, the debris burns up in the atmosphere. Streaks of light then fan out across the sky as a meteor shower.

There are about 30 meteor showers each year. Meteor showers are named after the **constellation** they seem to radiate from. The Perseid meteor shower is caused by a stream of dust left behind by the comet Swift-Tuttle. This shower appears mid-August in the **Northern Hemisphere**. First recorded in China 2,000 years ago, there can be more than 100 meteors in an hour.

METEORITES

Sometimes a meteor is large enough that it does not burn up in Earth's atmosphere. A meteor that strikes Earth is called a meteorite. Meteorites can be as small as a pebble and as large as a massive boulder. In 1991, two boys in Indiana heard an odd whistling sound. Moments later, they saw a meteorite hit the ground not far from where they were standing. It was about the size of a baseball. Scientists at Purdue University studied this meteorite. They discovered it broke off an asteroid about 45 million years ago!

Another annual meteor shower is the Leonids. This meteor shower is named for the constellation Leo. The Leonids appear each November when Earth's orbit takes it through the dust trail of Comet Tempel-Tuttle. This comet enters the inner solar system every 33 years. In 902 CE, the Leonids were first recorded by Chinese astronomers.

Usually, people see 10 to 15 bright meteors per hour. But some years, the Leonid shower makes it look like it is raining light. In 1833, sky watchers observed hundreds of thousands of meteors fall per hour! In 1966, the Leonids were even more spectacular. Some people compared the meteor shower to a waterfall. At one point during the shower, there were as many as 40 meteors per second!

ANCIENT METEORITE CRATERS

Have you ever looked at the moon on a clear night? You may have noticed lots of meteorite craters. Earth has massive craters, too, about 180 of them. In 2012, scientists discovered the oldest crater on Earth near the town of Maniitsoq in Greenland. They believe it is more than 3 billion years old.

Before the discovery of the Maniitsoq crater, the Vredefort Dome in South Africa was thought to be the oldest crater. More than 2 billion years ago, a meteorite the size of a mountain slammed into this area of South Africa. When the meteorite exploded, it blasted away rock and dust, creating three rings. The outer ring is 186 miles wide.

Did You Know?

More meteorites are found in Antarctica than anywhere else in the world. This is not because more meteorites land there. One reason is dark meteorites stand out on Antarctica's snowy landscape. The snow and ice also help to preserve these space rocks.

A RECORD BREAKER

The Barringer Crater is near Flagstaff, Arizona. It is also called the Meteor Crater. Scientists think a meteorite the size of a 16-story building slammed into the Arizona desert about 50,000 years ago. Traveling at about 9 miles a second, the meteorite's impact tossed out 100 million tons of rock. It created a bowl-shaped crater nearly a mile wide and 600 feet deep. It is so large that 20 football games could be played in it at the same time!

DEADLY ASTEROIDS

About 65 million years ago, a meteorite from an asteroid larger than Mount Everest crashed into the Yucatan Peninsula in Mexico. The giant meteorite created a crater 6 miles wide. It is called the Chicxulub Crater. Many scientists believe that this asteroid began a series of events that led to the end of the dinosaurs.

Scientists think the collision violently shook Earth. It triggered terrible earthquakes and volcanic eruptions. The force of the blast produced a cloud of rock and dust that might have blocked the sun for months. Without the sun, most plants would have died out. As a result, most of life on Earth died, including the dinosaurs.

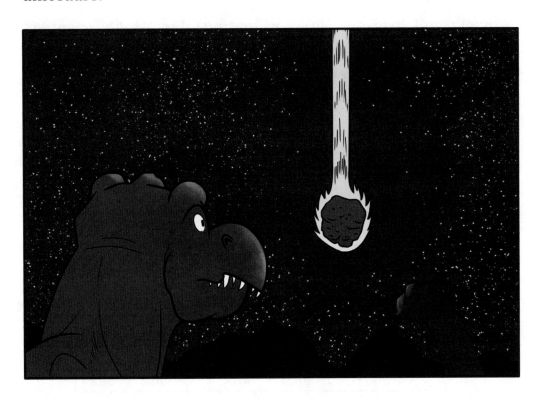

In 2016, scientists drilled into the Chicxulub Crater and pulled out layers of broken and melted rock from the time of the impact. Researchers are still studying the rocks. Will the scientists discover evidence of life after the impact? We will have to wait and see.

WHERE DOES AN ASTRONAUT DOCK HIS SPACECRAFT?

HA HA HA HA HA

At a parking meteor.

Could a massive asteroid like the one that created the Chicxulub Crater come close to Earth? It's unlikely in your lifetime. But because of the potential danger from asteroids and comets, NASA watches objects with orbits that bring them within 45,000 million miles of Earth. These objects are called Near Earth Objects (NEOs). Scientists study NEOs to make sure they won't hit our planet.

Comets and asteroids are fascinating objects! As scientists develop better ways of finding and visiting comets and asteroids, we learn more about what they have that we could use and what clues they have about the beginning of the solar system. Heads up!

Did You Know?

The International Space Station flies in a low orbit around Earth. To protect it from meteors and meteoroids, the station has a type of armor called the Whipple shield. The shield protects the station and crew from space debris up to 1 inch wide.

? CONSIDER AND DISCUSS

It's time to consider and discuss: What can ancient craters tell us about the history of Earth?

WATCH THE PERSEIDS

The Perseids are one of the most popular meteor showers to watch. They occur each August in the Northern Hemisphere. Look up the exact dates of this meteor shower or other showers at the American Meteor Society's website here.

KEYWORD PROMPTS

meteor shower calendar 🔍

1 Consult with the meteor shower calendar and set your chair up outside early in the morning, before the sun is up.

2 Plan on watching the sky for at least an hour. You don't want to miss this show! Count the number of meteors you see. Will you see three or 100?

3 Watch the Perseid meteor shower each morning for several days. Keep track of your observations in your science scroll. Put your results into a bar graph to keep track of how many meteors you see.

TRY THIS! Try collecting micrometeorites in your backyard. Place a plastic tray outside during the week of the Perseid meteor shower. After a week, place a strong magnet in a sandwich bag and run it over the material collected on the tray. Examine the material sticking to the magnet with a microscope. Perhaps you will have discovered some tiny space rocks?

PROJECT!

MAKE METEOR CRATERS

Every day, asteroids approach Earth. Most asteroids burn up in Earth's atmosphere. But larger asteroids sometimes make it to Earth's surface and make craters on impact. There are about 180 known craters on Earth. In this experiment, you will make and compare craters.

SUPPLIES

* science scroll
* pencil
* ruler
* newsprint
* baking pan
* 2 cups flour (must cover bottom of pan)
* ruler
* chocolate pudding mix
* sifter
* small objects to represent meteors, such as raisins, nuts, or grapes

1 In your science scroll, make a chart with 4 columns and 5 rows.

2 Along the top of the chart above each column write the following: "Object," "Object Diameter," "Crater Diameter," and "Crater Depth." Place the science scroll to one side.

3 Spread out the newsprint to keep your experiment station neat. Place the pan on top of the newsprint. Pour the flour into the bottom of the pan. Add enough flour to completely cover the bottom to a depth of 1 to 2 inches. Use your ruler to check this measurement. Shake the baking pan to level the flour.

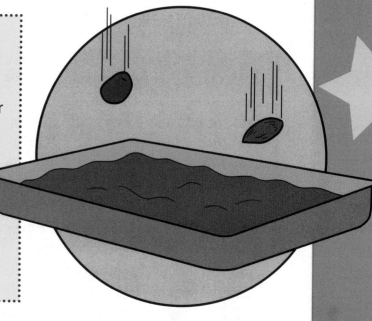

78

4 Use a sifter to cover the flour with a thin layer of pudding mix.

5 Drop one object at a time from the same height into the flour mixture. After each drop, measure the depth and diameter of the crater with your ruler. Write your results on your chart.

6 Look at your results. At the bottom of the chart, write down the average diameters and depths of the craters.

THINK ABOUT IT: Do you think the experiment would change if you dropped the objects from a greater or lower height? Make a prediction and test your results.

TRY THIS! Craters are rare on Earth because of many factors, such as our planet's atmosphere and weather. See for yourself the effect of weather on craters by filling a spray bottle with water. Turn the nozzle to mist and spray your craters several times. Observe what happens and think about how it might affect craters over hundreds of millions of years.

THEN & NOW

THEN: A dagger found wrapped alongside Egyptian King Tutankhamun was made with iron from a meteorite.

NOW: Meteorites provide scientists with information about the early solar system.

PROJECT!

FRICTION

Friction causes meteors to burn up in the atmosphere. You can discover how friction affects objects in this simple experiment.

1 Lightly touch a smooth surface with your finger such as a tabletop. Begin to move your finger back and forth quickly.

2 Press down firmly with your finger and move it rapidly back and forth. What do you feel?

3 Write down your observations in your science scroll.

4 Now, touch the flat surface with four of your fingers. Gently move them back and forth.

5 Press your fingers down firmly, and move them rapidly back and forth.

6 Did your results vary when you pressed down on the surface with more force? Explain your answer and record your observations in your science scroll.

TRY THIS! Learn more about how friction affects moving objects. Try rolling a toy car or ball along sandpaper, tile, and carpet. Which material slowed down the object the most? Which material slowed down the object the least?

GLOSSARY GAME

Pick up a pencil and get a friend or two to explore the ideas in this book by filling out this silly Mad Lib game.

- **noun:** a person, place, or thing
- **plural noun:** more than one person, place, or thing
- **adjective:** a word that describes a noun

- **verb:** an action word
- **adverb:** a word that describes a verb

STAR LIGHT, STAR BRIGHT

Star gazing is the best thing to do after sunset. On a clear night with

no _____ or _____, the stars are _____. This is your chance to
   NOUN   NOUN   ADJECTIVE

be an _____. This is a person who studies the planets, stars,
   NOUN

and other objects in the sky. Looking up into the sky, you spot

light _____.
  VERB

"Look!" you say. "There goes a _____."
                     NOUN

It is not a star, but a _____. Some of these _____ rocks are no
          NOUN   ADJECTIVE

larger than a grain of _____. As these rocks or pebbles enter
          NOUN

Earth's _____, they experience friction. Friction makes these rocks
    NOUN

or pebbles _____ brightly. You continue to follow the _____ as
      VERB   NOUN

it _____ toward Earth. If this rock had survived its fall through the
  VERB

atmosphere, it would have been a _____.
                         NOUN

archaeologist: a scientist who studies ancient people and their cultures through the objects they left behind.

asteroid: a small rocky object that orbits the sun.

astronomer: a person who studies the stars, planets, and other objects in space.

astronomical unit (AU): a unit of measure used in space. One AU is the average distance from the earth to the sun, 93 million miles.

astronomy: the study of the universe, especially the celestial bodies.

atmosphere: the blanket of air surrounding Earth.

basin: a hollow area of land surrounded by higher land.

BCE: put after a date, BCE stands for Before Common Era and counts down to zero. CE stands for Common Era and counts up from zero. These nonreligious terms correspond to BC and AD. This book was printed in 2017 CE.

carbon: an element found in living things, including plants. Carbon is also found in diamonds, charcoal, and graphite.

celestial body: a star, planet, moon, or other object in space, such as an asteroid or comet.

coincidence: a remarkable timing of events or circumstances without an apparent connection.

coma: an envelope of gases around a comet's nucleus.

comet: a ball of ice and dust that orbits the sun.

constellation: a group of stars in the sky that resembles a certain shape, such as the Big Dipper.

core: the innermost layer of a planet.

crater: a large hole in the ground caused by the impact of something such as a piece of an asteroid or a bomb.

culture: the beliefs and way of life of a group of people, which can include religion, language, art, clothing, food, holidays, and more.

element: a pure substance that cannot be broken down into a simpler substance. Everything in the universe is made up of combinations of elements. Oxygen and gold are two elements.

elliptical: shaped like an ellipse, or an oval.

flyby: a mission in which a spacecraft passes close to the object that is being studied.

foretold: predicted.

friction: the rubbing of one object against another.

geyser: a spring of water that, when heated, bursts into the air.

gravity: a force that pulls all matter together, including planets, moons, and stars.

horizon: the line in the distance where the land or sea seems to meet the sky.

Kuiper belt: a region of icy bodies beyond Neptune's orbit that includes Pluto and Eris. It is theorized that short period comets come from the Kuiper belt.

latitude: the angle of a location from the equator. The latitude is 0 degrees at the equator and 90 degrees at the North and South Poles.

lava: hot, melted rock that has risen to the surface.

long-period comet: a comet that takes more than 200 years to travel around the sun.

magnetic: having the properties of a magnet, capable of attracting metal.

main asteroid belt: an area of space between the orbits of Mars and Jupiter where most asteroids are found.

meteorite: a piece of space rock that falls to Earth.

meteoroid: a rock that orbits the sun. It is smaller than an asteroid and at least as large as a speck of dust.

meteor shower: when many pieces of dust burn up in Earth's atmosphere.

meteor: the streak of light when a bit of rock or dust enters Earth's atmosphere.

mineral: a naturally occurring solid found in rocks and in the ground. Rocks are made of minerals. Gold and diamonds are precious minerals.

mine: to dig something out of the ground.

mission: a scientific study of the solar system.

molecule: a group of atoms, which are the smallest particles of an element, bound together. Molecules combine to form matter.

myth: a traditional story about a hero or event.

near-Earth asteroids: asteroids that travel along orbits close to Earth.

Northern Hemisphere: the half of Earth north of the equator.

nucleus: the center of a comet. Plural is nuclei.

Oort Cloud: a collection of comets and icy material on the fringes of our solar system. It is theorized that long-period comets come from the Oort Cloud.

orbit: the path an object in space takes around a star, planet, or moon.

organic: of living things, or developing naturally.

philosopher: a person who thinks about and questions the way things are in the world and in the universe.

plasma tail: the hot, glowing gas tail of a comet.

prism: an object that disperses light and reflects it into the full color range of the rainbow.

probe: a spaceship or other device used to explore outer space.

quadrant: an instrument used to measure the height of the planets, moon, or stars.

resource: something that people can use.

short-period comet: a comet that takes less than 200 years to travel around the sun.

solar system: a family of eight planets and their moons that orbit the sun.

solar wind: the stream of electrically charged particles emitted by the sun.

spectra: bands of colors that a ray of light can be separated into. Singular is spectrum.

sublimation: when a solid turns to gas without first becoming a liquid.

telescope: a tool used to see objects that are far away.

Trojan asteroids: asteroids that share their orbits with larger objects in the solar system, such as planets.

Trojan War: a war fought between the ancient Greeks and the people of Troy around 1250 BCE.

METRIC CONVERSIONS

Use this chart to find the metric equivalents to the English measurements in this book. If you need to know a half measurement, divide by two. If you need to know twice the measurement, multiply by two. How do you find a quarter measurement? How do you find three times the measurement?

English	Metric
1 inch	2.5 centimeters
1 foot	30.5 centimeters
1 yard	0.9 meter
1 mile	1.6 kilometers
1 pound	0.5 kilogram
1 teaspoon	5 milliliters
1 tablespoon	15 milliliters
1 cup	237 milliliters

BOOKS

20 Fun Facts about Asteroids and Comets by Arielle Chiger and Adrienne Houk Maley (Gareth Stevens, 2014).

Exploring Comets, Asteroids, and Other Objects in Space by Nancy Dickmann (Rosen Central, 2015).

The Solar System, Meteors, and Comets by Clive Gifford (Crabtree, 2015).

Icy Comets: Sometimes Have Tails by Chaya Glaser (Bearport, 2015).

Comets by Nick Hunter (Heinemann Library, 2013).

Meteor Showers by J.A. Kelley (Children's Scholastic, 2010).

Comets by Kristen Rajczak (Gareth Stevens Pub., 2012).

Comets, Asteroids, and Meteorites by Carmel Reilly (Macmillan Library, 2011).

Across the Universe: Comets by Kate Riggs (Creative Paperbacks, 2015).

Meteors by Simon Rose (AV² by Weigl, 2011).

Exploring Dangers in Space: Asteroids, Space Junk, and More by Buffy Silverman (Lerner Publications, 2011).

The Lonely Existence of Asteroids and Comets by Mark Weakland (Capstone, 2012).

WEBSITES

Amazing Space:
amazingspace.org/resources/explorations

The Comets Tail-Berkeley:
cse.ssl.berkeley.edu/SegwayEd/lessons/CometsTale/com.html

Discovery Kids:
discoverykids.com/games/asteroid-comet-or-meteor-quiz

Enchanted Learning:
zoomschool.com/subjects/astronomy/comet

European Space Agency Kids:
esa.int/esaKIDSen/SEMN99WJD1E_OurUniverse_0.html

Images of Asteroids and Comets-NASA:
photojournal.jpl.nasa.gov/target/Other

Astronomy for Kids:
kidsastronomy.com/comets.htm

Kid's Cosmos:
kidscosmos.org/solar_system/asteroids_comets_meteors.php

National Geographic Kids-Comets:
kids.nationalgeographic.com/explore/space/comets

National Geographic Kids-Asteroids:
kids.nationalgeographic.com/explore/space/asteroids/#asteroid-belt.jpg

Nova-Doomsday Asteroid:
pbs.org/wgbh/nova/spacewatch

Solar System Exploration-NASA:
solarsystem.nasa.gov/planets

StarChild NASA-Comets:
starchild.gsfc.nasa.gov/docs/StarChild/solar_system_level1/comets.html

QR CODE GLOSSARY

Page 6: chroniclingamerica.loc.gov/lccn/sn85066387/1910-02-08/ed-1/seq-1

Page 11: earthexplorer.usgs.gov

Page 13: commons.wikimedia.org/wiki/File:PIA20041-Asteroid-2015TB145-Animation-20151030.gif

Page 15: nasa.gov/mission_pages/neowise/images/index.html

Page 31: nssdc.gsfc.nasa.gov/photo_gallery/photogallery-asteroids.html

Page 52: sci.esa.int/rosetta/54704-comet-67p-on-24-september-2014-navcam-mosaic

Page 55: nasa.gov/mission_pages/sunearth/news/comet-lovejoy.html

Page 64: hubblesite.org/gallery/album/solar_system/kuiper_belt_object

Page 67: static1.squarespace.com/static/519e5c43e4b036d1b98629c5/t/5277d5a3e4b0bef5deee712b/1383585187053/Making+the+Ellipse+-+C37.pdf

Page 77: amsmeteors.org/meteor-showers/meteor-shower-calendar

ESSENTIAL QUESTIONS

Introduction: Do people worry about comets and asteroids today the way they did in historical times? Why or why not?

Chapter 1: Why do asteroids come in many different shapes and sizes?

Chapter 2: Why were asteroids hard to study in the past? Why are we interested in studying them now?

Chapter 3: How can asteroids be useful to people on Earth?

Chapter 4: Why did people fear comets in the past? Why aren't most people afraid of them now?

Chapter 5: Why do we study objects that we might not be able to see within our lifetime?

Chapter 6: What can ancient craters tell us about the history of Earth?